a place to
grow

edited by

DAVID HASSLER
LYNN GREGOR

photography by

DON SNYDER

a place to grow

voices and images *of urban gardeners*

The Pilgrim Press
Cleveland, Ohio

The Pilgrim Press, Cleveland, Ohio 44115

Text © 1998 by David Hassler and Lynn Gregor

Photography © 1998 by Don Snyder

All rights reserved. Published 1998

Printed in Hong Kong on acid-free paper

03 02 01 00 99 98   5 4 3 2 1

Library of Congress Cataloging-in-Publication Data

A place to grow : voices and images of urban gardeners / edited by David Hassler and Lynn Gregor ;

  photography by Don Snyder.

    p.   cm.

  Includes bibliographical references.

  ISBN 0-8298-1295-4 (alk. paper)

  1. Community gardens—United States—Anecdotes.   2. Gardeners—United States—Anecdotes.   3. Gardening—

United States—Anecdotes.

I. Hassler, David, 1964–   .   II. Gregor, Lynn, 1971–   .

SB457.3.P555   1998

635′.092′273—dc21   98-22405

                                                                                    CIP

contents

foreword

*W*e didn't start our garden with much. We didn't have much—no fancy tools or sheds, boots or compost bins. What we did have was all that mattered: land and people, work and hands. Out of rubble and garbage, we began to grow a garden, but not just a garden. As one participant, George Williams, says, "We grow people too."

The neighborhood where our garden is located isn't featured on any postcards of San Francisco. It is on a large stretch of land that you see to the left of the highway when driving into the city. It is typical, urban poor/lower-income America—where work disappears, where the city sends its refuse (both human and material), where there are more liquor stores than libraries or safe green spaces, and where decades of promises and initiatives have created lots of photo opportunities for politicians, but little change.

San Francisco, of course, is not alone in its problems of poverty, nor is it alone in the fact that its poor neighborhoods also lack parks and trees. Across the country, trees and green spaces are commensurate with income. In 1987, the Reverend Benjamin Chavis, then director of the

Commission for Racial Justice of the United Church of Christ, oversaw a report on environ-mental racism which found a pattern of concentrating uncontrolled hazardous waste facilities in minority communities; three out of five black and Hispanic Americans and almost half of all Asian/Pacific Islanders and Native Americans live in such communities. In 1992, the *National Law Journal* found efforts by federal pollution cleanup programs to be fewer, slower, and less thorough in minority communities, and polluters were fined less often.

The result of living in such environments, besides higher rates of asthma and cancers, is that people have little knowledge of the earth beneath the concrete. People ask me why our garden isn't vandalized; sadly, it's because many of our neighbors do not know that food can come from the earth, not just from a supermarket shelf or a frozen-food section. The other effects of living in such environments are far more complicated than anyone can explain. But we know the com-mon symptoms—gangs, crime, high rates of dropouts, poor schools, joblessness—all of which amount to social, emotional, and physical chaos.

In *A Continuous Harmony,* poet, novelist, and essayist Wendell Berry writes, "Out of a his-tory so much ruled by the motto Think Big, we have come to a place and a need that requires us to think little." In many ways, our program here in San Francisco began as Father Jim O'Donnell of Cleveland began his garden. He says: "The corner where we have that park called 'Oasis of Peace' was filled with rocks and glass and junk. Somehow it reflected the neighbor-hood, and it reflected how people felt. In my own heart I'm thinking, let's turn that corner into a garden of love. Let's put flowers and plants and trees in there, so that people see one pocket, one little place that says, it's beautiful, and everything isn't junk down here, and we're not all junk—we're not all to be thrown away."

When we first began our garden, no newspaper reporters or politicians came out to see what we were doing. We started with seeds and dirt. Now we have jobs, good food, an awareness of our immediate and extended environment, a place where seniors come to spend their days and where children run, play, and gather snails in their pockets. One of the most common observations from our seniors is that they used to fear the young people who work in our garden. Those young people were afraid too. Somewhere during those days spent quietly working the earth, seeing a previously unknown cycle of growth and renewal, nurturing and persistence, something is released and something changes. People ask me what I tell these young people to inspire and support them. I say, I don't—it's working with green things that does. So we grow people too.

And those people grow other people. They bring their families and friends to our garden. They bring the food they grow home to their families and communities. They are proud to sell their food at farmers' markets, and to explain to customers the different kinds of lettuce we grow. We didn't know what we were doing when we began our garden, we only knew we had to begin somewhere. Beginning somewhere is enough: the economist E. F. Schumacher once wrote,

"Perhaps we cannot raise the winds. But each of us can put up the sails so that when the wind comes we can catch it."

Inner cities in America are not the only places that need gardens; cities as a whole need gardens. By the year 2000 more than 50 percent of the world's population will live in cities. Cities are more crowded. Skyscrapers are taller. Office buildings and complexes seem to appear in a matter of weeks. As cities expand, the green spaces within them are more and more neglected. Let us remember what William Faulkner observed more than forty years ago: "They call this progress, but they don't say where it's going." We can see where it's going: urban dwellers are mentally and physically caught in its ebb and flow, rarely interacting with those different from themselves, much less the earth beneath the concrete. Work and home are individual and family affairs.

More and more, we lack connection to the earth and community. The degradation of the environment is not new; the statistics are by now familiar, the need only more urgent. The other need, the human need for community, is just as urgent. Cities need places which bring people together and engage them with one another. We can create such places without much, or, rather, with what we've had all along: land and people, work and hands. The stories in *A Place to Grow: Voices and Images of Urban Gardeners* testify to the power of green space.

Nationally, people are beginning to heed such calls. The American Community Gardening Association estimates that there are between 250 and 500 citywide gardening programs. Schools, private businesses, and government agencies are all beginning to realize the benefits of growing gardens: gardens offer children hands-on learning, places of solace in our work environments, chances for rehabilitation of the sick and incarcerated, jobs in communities sorely in need of them. Citizens are organizing to revive neglected parks. Urban farmers' markets are growing and thriving. The organic food market is the fastest-growing market in the agricultural sector. We're learning that we really *are* what we eat and where we live, and that we're better when we eat well and when we live amid more than just concrete, brick, and stucco. Communities, the social and physical environment, are better too.

So we're starting to think little. All around this country, communities are putting up their sails. Because we need to grow people too. It's about time.

Cathrine Sneed has been gardening with prisoners since 1984 on an eight-acre organic farm at the San Francisco County Jail. In 1992 she founded The Garden Project, which employs ex-prisoners who grow and sell organic produce to local restaurants and bakeries. She recently started two new programs: The Tree Corps hires ex-prisoners and people from local neighborhoods to plant trees in those neighborhoods; The School Corps teaches students to plant gardens and beautify school grounds in low-income neighborhoods. Her pioneer work with disadvantaged people has been instrumental in helping to start similar programs in schools and other cities. In 1997 the United States Department of Agriculture documented her programs in a widely distributed booklet, *The Garden Project.* Considered a national leader in this field, Cathrine Sneed has been invited throughout the country to speak about her experiences. Her work and the stories she tells have been an inspiration for this book.

David Hassler & Lynn Gregor

acknowledgments

acknowledgments

We are grateful to Cultivating Our Community, Ohio State University Extension's urban gardening program in Cuyahoga County, which has generously provided us with materials, time, and guidance. A special thanks to Dennis Rinehart, extension agent in urban gardening, Kathleen O'Neill, development coordinator, and Mary Kay Girton, program manager. From the beginning they believed in and supported the project. We also thank the city of Cleveland's Summer Sprout program for over twenty-five years of supporting urban gardeners.

We are grateful to our good friends Ted Lyons and Pauline Thornton for their invaluable comments and careful readings of the manuscript, Jeff St. Clair and Mark Brazaitis for their support and encouragement, and Michael Lyons for his expert advice.

Thanks to our editors, Timothy Staveteig and Marjorie Pon, to the art director, Martha Clark, who made this book a visual feast, and to the entire Pilgrim Press staff for their help.

We especially thank Don Snyder, who immediately shared our enthusiasm for the project and whose photographs beautifully portray the spirit of the gardeners.

We are grateful to the gardeners themselves, who graciously brought us into their homes and lives. There are so many more whose stories do not appear in these pages. We are honored by their trust and friendship. We offer this book in thanks to all urban gardeners throughout the country whose hard work and commitment brings hope to our lives and to our cities.

David Hassler & Lynn Gregor

XIII

acknowledgments

the gardeners

voices

Annie Browning, Steve Cernan, Emmanuel Delgado,

Tommy Dorsey, Julie Jackson, Linda Jakob, Dan Kane, Eugene Mattox,

Gustina Nicholas, Father Jim O'Donnell, Brenda Taylor-Rosario,

Maggie Walsh-Conrad, Dorothy Zeigler

prologue

look around and I say, "You know from a few little seeds look what's come. Out of nothing, look what's come!" It takes time, that's all, it takes time. You all know that with the garden, everything you plant doesn't come up right away.

Did you ever read the story about the man who planted trees in France? It's a beautiful story. Around 1917 this man, very young at the time, was living alone, a life of solitude, in this barren, windy, stormy place in France. Every day he would go out and plant little acorns. He went all the way through World War I without ever knowing there was a World War I. Planes were overhead in World War II and he didn't know what they were up there for. He was still planting. Every day he planted little acorns as part of his balance between being quiet and doing his physical work.

Somewhere in his late eighties, he had planted a hundred thousand acorns. And now today there stands a forest in France with ten thousand trees. What was barren now has water, life, a forest—ten thousand trees! This man humbly, and in a very quiet way, planted those seeds every day. Through all those years, through two world wars, until he was well into his eighties, he was still planting those acorns.

Out of that nothingness and that fidelity, nobody to encourage him, he just did it. Out of his love for God? For quiet? Before that, in villages around there, people were living chaotic lives, they were quarreling and fighting and drinking. Gradually, as this forest began to grow, it changed all the environments around it. The people began to find life. It changed their whole way of life. They weren't living the way they were before. New life came into the people, as well as into the forest.

And so in trees and flowers and plants—in gardens—something brings life and it affects people inside. It helps them hope. It makes for a better life. You can build a new house and still, internally, nothing may change. And if it doesn't change, then things aren't going to be okay.

The city gardening program has been a tremendous help, because it has encouraged us so and made everything possible. Everything to help you and teach you and show you. With that kind of help, how could you not do it? And above all, most of the gardens are all in the inner city, in the urban areas. They're bringing life to a place that for many people was very blighted.

a good

beginning

*T*he way our garden got started? Honestly, one day in 1978 my mother was sitting on the porch, and these two dogs would always come in front of her porch to do their business. She said, "Brenda, we're gonna put a fence up!" So what we done–my mother, Emma Taylor, my sons, Temujin and Temartus, and I—we put up a fence in front of her yard. And she said, "Come on, let's go to the graveyard and get some leaves." We went to the graveyard on 65th Street, brought leaves, truckloads of leaves, and built our front yard up. Then my sister, Florence, she said, "Well, that's growing pretty good, 'cause them flowers are looking beautiful." So she and my brother, Rufus, put a fence up on their side of the yard and it just caught on like wildfire. Everybody up and down 61st Street wanted flowers in their yard.

One day Reverend Mary Beech came, and we were walking down the street together, and she said, "Brenda, you see all these wine and whiskey bottles all in between the houses?" It was dirty and I says, "I just can't live like this, I can't live like this!" So we started cleaning up. We cleaned up our whole neighborhood. Lonnie Burton was our councilman then. He say, "You know something? You all are really doing something good around here." Then the city got involved, and Reverend Beech introduced Mrs. Hazel Pruitt. She was the head of the city gardening program for our area down here. She brought me plants and she'd say, "Brenda, just put it in the ground, it will grow!" That's what she would always say to me, "Just put it in the ground, it will grow."

t's just a transformation now from what it was then. The corner where we have that park called "Oasis of Peace" was filled with rocks and glass and junk. Somehow it reflected the neighborhood, and it reflected how people felt. In my own heart I'm thinking, let's turn that corner into a garden of love. Let's put flowers and plants and trees in there, so that people see one pocket, one little place that says, it's beautiful, and everything isn't junk down here, and we're not all junk—we're not all to be thrown away.

There were so many older men at that time that hung out down at the park. They have all gone now, most of them have died, actually. They were all alcoholics. They were people who'd spent anywhere from ten to twenty years in prison and just were down in life, just didn't find much meaning to their life. My way of becoming one with them one day was to go up there—they were all drinking their beer or wine out of their brown paper bags, and they knew I didn't drink. So one guy bought me a Coke and put it in a brown paper bag and said, "Here you are, rev baby." So I drank that day with them. It was great. That garden became a place where I, at least for a while, could take the bottle out of one hand and put the shovel in the other hand. And that was a wonderful gift.

I found that a lot of these men were especially gifted. Some of them had been construction workers, some had been carpenters, and some of them had been really good laborers. When I would go to do things, they'd tell me, that's not the way you do it! And it wasn't, and I didn't know! I thought, great, you show me, I just want you here.

voices

"So there's always somebody trying to make it a little bit better. The whole idea was to help people feel that they're good. People are good."

A friend of mine built all those benches around the trees, because when these trees grow up there'll be shade here. When you put a little tree in, you can't imagine how big it's going to get, or how it's going to throw any shade. But now that they're up there, and the benches are around the trees, it's perfect. Many times as it gets hot in the summer, you'll find people going there to sit, just thinking to themselves.

So there's always somebody trying to make it a little bit better. The whole idea was to help people feel that they're good. People *are* good. As one man said, "I really thought that I was nothing, but when I see people like you and Sister Maggie come down here, I feel God must have sent you to tell me I'm a good person." I said, "That's right. That's the only reason we're here." So that's how we began, and this has evolved over the years. I didn't know a thing about gardening, you know. I never gardened in my life.

I was assigned to the Broadway Outreach Center, Cleveland Police Department, in 1973. We were asked to get the community involved in different projects. I would go around to the senior citizen groups and to the schools in the neighborhood and talk about crime prevention programs. And this thought came to my mind, that when I was a kid, my dad and I had a little plot of ground on Canal and Warner Roads. We'd go out there a couple times a week, about a four-mile walk. We'd get water from the canal and water the garden.

When I was at the Outreach Center I had to get some programs together, so I thought it'd be a good idea to get the kids in the neighborhood involved in gardening. We had an empty lot here that was used as a football practice field at one time. I got permission from the city to use it as a garden site for kids to grow vegetables.

The first year we had our garden was 1974. Mayor Perk was driving by the garden with his son, who was a councilman in the Fifteenth Ward, and said, "What's going on here?" Our garden was in full bloom. "That's a hell of a good idea!" he said. So in 1976 Mayor Perk started the Summer Sprout program for the city.

"I thought it'd be a good idea
to get the kids in the neighborhood
involved in gardening."

really started gardening when I moved here around 1960. I started in the back, and I really started loving it. I'd lived around farms all my life. I never lived on a farm, but I always loved it—the idea of a farm. I started here with just a little patch. I had beans, greens, and tomatoes. I had peppers, hot peppers. It's like filling a void in your life—something you know but can't put together until you start. It's a part of my routine, a part of my life. Not that I'm a fanatic farmer now, but I like doing it.

My people down South, they always had gardens. This is how they survived during the Depression years. They had gardens, they had chickens and pigs—even in the city. Actually, a lot of my people were starving. But you know, they say necessity is the mother of invention. That's an intellectual way to say it. When you get down to it, you throw the book away and you say, look, I have to have food.

So I've been around this planting and harvesting all my life, although, like I say, the first time I ever planted a garden was here. I threw away the rocks and bricks and everything else you see piled out there. I said, I'm gonna dig this up and put a garden here. Everything came up beautiful. I told my wife, I said, "Look at some of these beans!" She went and cooked them right up. I said, "These beans taste good. They're good!" Then I started realizing I'd had fresh beans before. It was like a throwback to when I was a child and they used to cook stuff directly out of the garden. You go to the store and you buy beans—they've been there two or three days or a week. Oh, they're green, but there's a difference!

'd never put the Summer Sprout sign up except the day they came to plow. The reason why is the word "community." They thought they were supposed to come in and get everything. I learned people think community means freebies. This lady with her little kid came around the corner from the next street. She was pulling him in a little red wagon. She come around, put the greens in the wagon. I saw the greens were on top. The bad thing was, she made the kid pull the wagon. She was holding the kid's hand. I said to her, "Didn't you just get those out of the garden?" She said, "Yeah." "Don't you know you have to be part of the garden?" I said, "Come to 12815 St. Clair meeting. Put up ten dollars. Now you become a part of that. Don't you see those little stakes? Don't you see you went in everybody's garden? What am I gonna tell them?"

"Now I don't mind you subsidizin' but . . ." She smiled. I said, "You see, the only time you steal is when you feel like you stole. I didn't call it stealin'—I said subsidizin'. Subsidizin' means you're gettin' something to help yourself. You have to pay these people back eventually." She's in the garden now! My grandmother always used to say you get people by sugar, you never get nothin' by pepper. I joke, I say to her child now, "You want to come back and subsidize?"

To get people to do things, all people, you have to manipulate them. The best way to manipulate anyone, if you want them to work, is to work with them. They always call me "the pusher." I never ask anyone to sweep the floor unless I sweep the floor. I worked as secretary of the church, and you ask anyone around about me. "She worked them to death," they'd say. I'd

"I don't meet strangers,

because there are

no strangers in my world."

"My grandmother always used to say
you get people by sugar,
you never get nothin' by pepper."

answer, "Oh no, I worked there with you!" When getting people to help in gardens, I always use the word "we." We, meaning you're a part of it. You can get a whole lot of projects started using we—"We start a row, we gonna plant seeds . . ."

Last summer we started the garden. So that got us growing together outside the church—out where I like to call it common ground. We get to know each other, to laugh and talk and joke. We always have jokes together. See, in church you're not as free unless it's coffee hour. I don't meet strangers, because there are no strangers in my world. None. We don't have to be at each other's house every day, but we have to have this closeness.

n, steve, tommy, brenda, doroth
tommy, brenda, dorothy, dan, stev

enda, dorothy, dan, steve, tomm
rothy, dan, steve, tommy, brend
n, steve, tommy, brenda, doroth

cultivating

community

We call this garden "the garden of love, hope, faith, and friendship." We say love for our neighbors, hope for our community, faith in God, and friendship for one another. One of the reasons why we came up with that motto for the garden was, at the time, when we first started the garden, the neighborhood was beginning to be really run-down. Buildings were deteriorating, and we thought that the garden would be a thing that would encourage folks to get involved and take more pride in the neighborhood. It has really improved the neighborhood and the community. Folks come by just to see the garden. Each year we don't have enough room to even provide a spot for the person who really would like to have a garden here.

One problem we had was with theft in the garden. People were kind of afraid, because they felt that someone would come in and steal their vegetables. I didn't think they would come in, but they do! So we told the people: "You plant enough for the thief and yourself and enough for the birds."

There was a man out here that was takin' the vegetables. One of our gardeners looked at the other one and said, "Who is that?" "That's the thief Mrs. Zeigler told us would come out here!" And instead of tellin' him to leave, he said, "Mrs. Zeigler said plant enough for the thief, and that's the thief out here gettin' his share." So we've had much fun.

Most of the gardeners keep their garden up and take pride in it. It's not like a job, it's a pride. It's one of the greatest things that's ever happened to this community to improve it. And those new homes over there, I think the garden had a lot to do with them comin'.

This garden thing took me. In a garden no one has anything that the other guy can't have. You can all have what you want. When I grow tomatoes, everybody has tomatoes. The vegetables and the produce we get we give to three different hunger centers in the area. Down 65th Street there's a hole in the fence there about yea big. I'll see somebody walking by, and I'll say, "A tomato, ma'am? A tomato, mister?" They say, "Yeah, sure." So I go up to the hole and hand 'em the tomatoes. The hole in the fence, I call it my ATM!

A lot of people that walk by ask, "Can we get into the garden?" If we have space we'll give them a garden. The people get together and they share with one another ideas or what's going on in the neighborhood. It's real nice. We like to say: "Every city dweller should have a place in the country, even if it's in the city."

In 1975 we had our first Harvest Dance. I had top polka bands come in there. They'd donate seven to nine. Bajelic, Tiresky, Wally Polkachips. He was number one! He died probably about three or four years ago. Top, top polka band. I had a friend who was in the trucking business and he would bring a flatbed in there for a stage, right inside the garden on the asphalt. We had beer donated for the adults and pop for the kids. We'd put straw on the asphalt and people did their polkas! They danced!

t started a good many years ago. I was asked to serve on the Hunger Task Force Committee at West Side Ecumenical Ministry. I said my expertise was gardening, so I suggested we put in more gardens for people and let them grow food to supplement their food budget. I went to all the community gardens to see what they were doing and everything was just a hodgepodge, everybody gardening their own way and no system. So I was compelled to start a garden here.

I got permission from Governor Rhodes and the state highway department, which owns the land. They'll let you use any land on the highway as a community garden if it's available. I could pay rent on this land and go private. But as long as it's a community garden, you don't have to pay for anything. There are millions of acres available.

So I set up this garden, strictly organic. The concept was less work, less cost, a more productive way of gardening. Low-income people can't afford to buy plant material, fertilizers, pesticide, things like that. Nothing's been put on that garden except leaves and grass that are thrown away every day—it makes a good amendment. We have one of the finest gardens in the country. It hasn't been fertilized in five years, because we keep changing crops and techniques. Otherwise, we let the worms do all the work. After all these years I've got humus, that thick, beautiful soil.

When I started this program I wanted to do like they were doing for seven thousand years in China and in Europe. Growing intensely, no-till, everything returned to the earth. I can get a

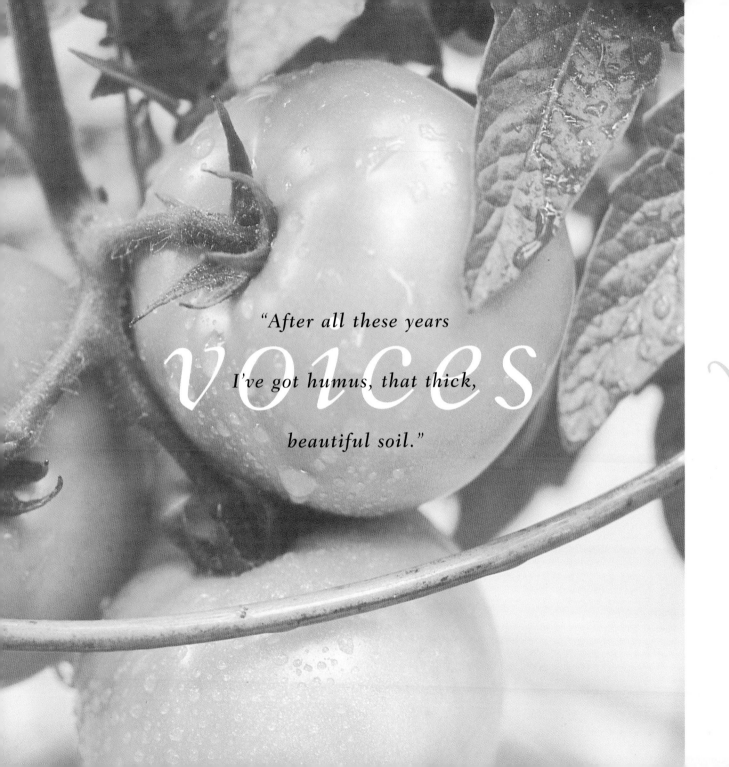

"After all these years

voices

I've got humus, that thick,

beautiful soil."

low-income family and if they follow this concept and are willing to work it, they could make over $40,000 a year. Now you see, that's hard to believe. But if I can do it, they can do it. I mean I'm no miracle man, you know—it's all in the soil.

What we want is an eating garden. We want to start eating and eat twelve months out of the year. We have garlic and onions all winter and sometimes carrots we cover with leaves. You want better quality in life, then go into an organic garden. You're going to get it from there, you're going to get better quality. I'll be eighty-one years old, and I've been to a doctor twice in eighteen years. I've eaten out of the garden all these years. That's what I attribute my health to— that and the work I do in the garden.

would love to see this gardening program happen, especially in "the bricks." It's a great educational tool. You can't find an individual that will not be affected ultimately by a garden. I mean it could be helpful for everybody. What you have in these communities is people who are not in touch with the things of beauty. This would help for a total neighborhood renovation. I think it would be instrumental in reducing crime, because you're changing the way people think. And the way you can solve problems is changing the way people think. The garden is a common denominator for all people. It doesn't make any difference your social background, your economic background, how much money you got. We all have something in common in a garden. What better way to bridge any kind of gaps—it could be racial, it could be male and female. Everybody could come together on common ground. That's my opinion.

"We all have something in common in a garden. What better way to bridge any kind of gaps."

I ain't got much, but I ain't poor either, thank God. I thank God for that. I say it's only by the grace of God, that's why I live like I live. I want to uplift somebody! I can move away. I'll be glad to move away. But I'll always come back here to try to help somebody better themself.

It took seventeen years to get the garden up to where it is now. I want to buy the lot out there, but we have to pay our back taxes in order to get the lot. So I just take care of it in memory of Lonnie Burton and my dead father, Theodore Taylor, and all those that have passed on. I just try to keep it beautiful and fenced in. And the birds and the squirrels, everything—they come here like it's a sanctuary.

People come down here, and they look and say, "I want to be married out there in the garden." This one man told me, "I want to be buried in your garden." I say, "You can't be buried out there!" But I say, "I love you, George."

The way I look at it, I try to have pink flowers there. In our environment there's so much violence going on, I try to have things where the children can come and look and say, "Hmm, something different's going on around here. How come she don't live like what they're doing around here? She don't live like that." And see that's a witness to them—you don't have to be like that. You don't have to do drugs. You don't have to be drinking. You don't have to be smoking. They get back home to their parents and they be acting like, "Momma and Daddy, why you be doing that? Ms. Taylor doesn't do that." That's a witness to them to try to uplift them.

"I try to have things where the children

voices

can come and look and say, 'Hmm,

something different's going on around here.' "

I appreciate everybody that is working with the city gardening program. They're helping people that are poor. We teach them how to grow their own and uplift themselves. I save over $500 a year just on food alone. I been givin' food away for at least fifteen years. They say, "Ms. Taylor, you got anything?" I just let them go in my garden and get what they want. I do. I love them. But you know how some people is, they don't want to do nothin'! I'd give them some plants and seeds just to try to help themselves. They'd rather come and get, than to work. You know how they are. I don't want to talk about them, God forgive me. But I try to encourage them.

I could have moved away from here years ago. I could have been gone! But I just stay here to try to uplift somebody. That's why I stay here. I got money, I could have been gone. But like Reverend Beech told me, she said, "Brenda, God has a plan for you. It's the reason why you be where you be. It's the reason why." You know, I can go away, I can run. But these people down here, they need somebody to be a leader. My mother say, "Be a leader, you can show people." That's why I stay. You can uplift somebody just by the way you live.

the growing

season

*T*here's a child that says, can I help you? Can I do something? It's very important that we try to help them and respond to that. If they want to do it, let's teach them something. Maybe they won't stay with it, but that's all right. I can't help but feel that we all remember those good things. You grow up with them and you don't forget them. And the children won't forget them.

I think the most important thing with children is the relationship they have with an adult. They're doing something with you and they enjoy that. I had a youngster here last summer and I had this little tool for rooting out the weeds, like a little mattock. So I had this little fellow, and I said, "Now today we're going to plant." I forget what I was planting, it might have been beans. I showed him how to plant these things. He wanted that tool I had! He said, "I know how to do that, I know how to use that!" I had a feeling he didn't, but he was not about to stay planting. He wanted that tool as bad as . . . worse than I did. So I ended up giving him the tool, and my God, I thought he was going to rip up half the garden! But he loved it like an eight-year-old. He enjoyed whacking away with that thing. So it's little things like that.

Sometimes you have to be patient and help them and teach them. I think that above all, at the end of the day, they'll remember that they were with you. It's also good for me, because I discover the wisdom of the child. They ask you all kinds of questions. It's a place where you can talk, and the child can ask questions that they wouldn't in the house. It's a relationship I have with the child and the child with me that I don't have any other way. So many of our children

"I find that the kids I have the best

voices

relationship with today are those that come and

work with me in the garden."

here are really parenting themselves. They don't have somebody who's going to sit down and talk with them and be with them. They just love it when they go out in the garden with you. I find that the kids I have the best relationship with today are those that come and work with me in the garden. Over the years, I see the garden has been the instrument in working with the child.

When we moved here, it was an all African American neighborhood. The neighbors were curious about what we were about. We didn't set out to do anything but just to live here. It was the children that kind of announced us. After being here a few years, one of the little children said, "Sister Maggie, why do my parents call you guys the white folks?" They never saw color. It's not an issue until they get older, in the higher grades, and they learn other things about prejudice, and it becomes an awareness, a reality for them about black and white.

We've had the greenhouse maybe four years now. A friend of ours from Avon who is a farmer helped us build it. It's a place where I work with the children. It's also been good for me, a place of contemplation. I realize what good therapy it is for me. I work with the children, teach them to plant the seed and to be responsible for watering it. The greenhouse gives them a role of responsibility and importance. They like coming away from their home to a place that's peaceful and quiet.

One time one of the children who had been here with us went home and had a disagreement with his parents. So he ran away from home. His parents called us to find out if he had come here. We hadn't seen him at all. We were on the watch for him all day Sunday. When I went out about five or six in the evening, he had been gone for a few hours. I happened to go out, probably to get Shadow, the dog, and noticed some movement. I went over and found him. He was in the greenhouse, weeping. I helped him realize that it was a good place to run away to, and that his tears had been a source of nurturing and had watered those plants. I also helped him to realize that he had to face the consequences of running away, and that I would accompany him to his parents' home. Because he ran to our greenhouse, I was able to be that middle person. When his parents were very angry and yelling and told him to go upstairs, I explained to them, didn't you ever run away? Don't you realize he was feeling unloved? It doesn't mean that he is unloved, but that's what he was experiencing and that was appropriate for his age.

I think the children here, as soon as they walk out their door, have to deal with the possibility of death, of an unsafe environment. It's a part of life—for them the whole world is that way. I think for most of them also, their own home environment is in chaos, it's a place of disorder. Coming to a place like this, a garden, brings a sense of order and rhythm, and escape from disorder and chaos. Most of the children I know are very bright but they lack a follow-up at home, a parent that's accompanying them with their schoolwork and saying, "Yes, you can do that." School becomes a negative place because they can't keep up. It can become a place of shame, and the children don't care whether they succeed or not. I keep telling them they can do well and they're really bright, but it's not consistent with the rest of their life.

I've come to enjoy gardening with them more and more. If we only help them a couple times a week with school-related things and they don't succeed, they feel they have failed. So I prefer

"Coming to a place like this, a garden,
brings a sense of order and rhythm,
and escape from disorder and chaos."

now to do things with the garden that aren't related to that type of success and failure. I always tell them to do your very best and do what you can. The grades you get aren't who you are. With gardening there's no sense of criticism, and they can see the fruit of their work.

Whenever they see me or Jim in the greenhouse or planting in the garden, they want to come and be a part of it. "Can I help you, Sister Maggie?" They just want to be with us. More important than what we're doing, they want to be a part of something where they feel valued, where they're helping and giving something.

The children we worked with when we first moved here are now in their thirties. They'll come back here and ask, "Sister Maggie, where's that photo album?" It's been a delight to me whenever they come back and want to recall those memories. We are like that other set of parents, in a sense. They'll bring a friend or fiancée and want to see those photos. So I know those experiences they had in the garden with us are very positive and life-forming. No matter what happens to them as adults, no matter where they end up, they have positive memories to recall from their childhood.

went around to different classrooms asking which kids might want to work in a summer gardening program. This was my mission, to see if I could get something going in the summertime with kids from the school, so that it would enable them to progress in their science learning by working in a garden over the summer. But also, because it was a real joyful activity for me. I remember I had fun working in my parents' garden when I was a kid. I think that getting back to the earth, working the land, is something that most kids are so out of touch with in the inner city. It seems just a waste that we have all this beautiful land where houses once stood. They are now dumping grounds that can be transformed into really beautiful places with just a little bit of effort.

This year, I wasn't going to be involved in the garden at all because I had a baby that was due in May. But she came early, and she died. She was three months premature. So, I kind of threw myself back into the garden thing again—it was really healing for me to do that.

I am not getting a stipend for being the school's garden leader. This is something I do out of love for the kids, love for the parents, and hopefully to give something back to the community. I consider myself pretty fortunate, and if I can teach and help people grow their own food for their families, or just for friends, and make it a fun activity, that's my reward.

Every time I drive in the city of Cleveland and I see an empty area of land I think, "Oh, that would make a nice garden." I mean, I'm looking for east-west exposure, I'm looking for the hydrant—it's contagious!

voices

"If I can teach and help people grow their own food for their families, or just for friends, and make it a fun activity, that's my reward."

We didn't have a contract when we came back to school last August. We were going to go on strike that Monday. But my main concern was what's going to happen to the tomatoes and the green peppers. I had to ask our union delegate person about all of the ramifications. If I'm on the picket line, would I be crossing the line if I opened the gate and watered or picked? Really, this is serious! I'm a union member and I'm pro-union, but I found ways around it if push came to shove. I would have died if I was walking the line and I saw these beautiful ripe tomatoes, and no one was able to eat them or pick them, and they were just dropping like flies.

*O*ur kids here at Children's Aid Society haven't really been cared for properly by any adults. No one has really cared for them. So I challenge them to take care of this eight-by-ten plot. I tell them, this is all yours, it's your responsibility and your piece of property. A lot of them haven't really owned a whole lot to begin with. It's up to me to teach them how to take care of their garden, and most of them do.

You're busy working, so it's a comfortable way to start talking with them and getting them to open up a bit. I haven't heard one unhappy memory about gardening come from the kids, unless it's to say, "My dad never let me in his garden, my dad never let me help." Maybe it's a fond memory of a grandma they would help pick the beans with, or a mother that taught them all about cutting up vegetables.

There was a boy who was new to the program that I didn't know very well. He was helping me cut up some vegetables, and he was a master chef, of course, because his mom taught him. You know, he hadn't seen his mom for a lot of years, but he remembered this. Gardening can bring out a lot of fond memories for our kids, no matter what their past is.

We had a little boy here who witnessed the murder of his father, and he had a lot of problems. If he wasn't really upset, he was generally very quiet. I didn't really know what was going on in his mind. For a couple years he kind of danced around the garden, really didn't do much, sort of avoided it by misbehaving when gardening time came up. Finally, in his third and fourth year, he started working in the program. But when he would have a pepper or a tomato or some-

thing, I was never seeing these things—they were always disappear-
ing. It turns out that he was burying them in the ground. Finally,
after I figured this out, he told me he was burying his vegetables,
because he wanted to see what happened to you when you died. This
was a way for him to work out the reality of what did happen to him
in his life.

That was a really big step for him to take, to actually face the death of his father and the
death of something that he had worked hard to grow. It was very therapeutic and safe, too. That
was so important for me to tell his therapists, because he would never talk about this, yet he was
working it out up there in the garden. Being a real quiet kid, he's not going to go up and say, hey,
I'm burying all my vegetables in my garden to see what happens to 'em. So it was a way for the
therapist to approach the child. That's why we call our gardening program a therapeutic program
here at Children's Aid Society.

You know if the kids can take care of a garden, they're feeling good about themselves. If I
have a girl come up here and she's planted seeds, and waited months for the flowers to grow, and
says to me, "Can I rip them out?" I know she's saying to me they're not good enough, and she's
not good enough. This is a girl that has an eating problem. She's not happy with herself, and she's
not happy with her garden either. The garden tells me a whole lot about how they're feeling
about themselves. For them to be able to take care of something means they're feeling pretty

good about themselves. They're confident. They can do it on their own. If they can do that on their own, they can do a whole lot more.

I love this job. I love gardening with the kids. You find yourself working and then you say, hey, this is nice, I feel peaceful. When you realize what it can do for you, you recognize when it's affected somebody else that same way. You remember the joy of growing carrots yourself as a kid and know that it's going to be just as exciting for them.

I remember the first year we grew potatoes here. When we started digging them up in the fall, the first potato we dug out was this big! I told the kids I'll take it home and see how it is. It's got to be full of bad spots and whatnot, I thought. I took it home and there wasn't a bad spot on it. And this was the first potato to grow. The kids just couldn't believe it. And the sweet potatoes were like that too. It was like buried treasure!

I know I've lost someone when he's got his weeds and he's going up to the compost pile and he stays up there. You look at him and he's on top of the mountain. He's on an adventure and he's jumping up and yelling at everybody. You've got to reel him back in. He's on the compost mountain. These kids are playing. That's what they need to do. But it's work at the same time, and they're having a blast.

Everything that I'm doing here, I've done with my mom. I kind of like being out, seeing all the greenery, having my hands dirty all the time. It's a nice experience, it's a way to relax. And plus, you put something in the ground and you watch it grow, like it's yours. Coming from a teenager, it sounds pretty funny, but it's really cool.

    Ever since I was a young boy, I always used to love going into the backyard with my mom, planting things, bringing home flowers from kindergarten, my mom helping me plant those in the backyard. That's what I really liked. My mom's been doing it all her life, ever since she was in Puerto Rico. That's her, that's my mom—the gardener.

    Others are exaggerating, if they think it's hard work. Come on, it's not like you didn't play with dirt when you were younger. But now you're doing something that you're going to get something out of.

    When Mr. Palange asks everybody in the program who wants to go to the garden, I automatically volunteer, 'cause I like coming here. It's better than being cooped up in the building. I'm in this program because of a violation of probation. A kid called me a "spic" and my temper just flew, my adrenalin started pumpin', and I broke his nose. That's why I'm here. I have to say I appreciate it a lot, because I know I would have gotten in trouble again if I wasn't in this program. I was acting like a jerk. Just a plain jerk. My mind was somewhere else. I wasn't being myself. I got in with the wrong crowd, did something I shouldn't have done.

"You put something in the ground and you watch it grow, like it's yours. Coming from a teenager, it sounds pretty funny, but it's really cool."

voices

"I'm happy about seeing my tomatoes grow, my peppers and cucumbers. I'm happy to know that they're actually alive."

When you have nothin' to do—comin' from a teenager—anything is on the list: fighting, going out and getting drunk, going out and getting high. All that stuff is there for you to do. But when you're doing something else that is going to occupy your mind, and you know that it's not bad, you know it's good—you really don't got to worry about it. You barely even think about it. I don't even think about drinkin', going out beating people up. I have other things to think about.

I'm happy about seeing my tomatoes grow, my peppers and cucumbers. I'm happy to know that they're actually alive. Now it's growing and it's like, wow, it's working out! And they're growing so fast. That's what's really surprising.

A couple of weeks ago when we came to the garden, I was having problems with this kid named Bobby, a short, cocky kid. Me and him were having some problems when we came here. After workin' in the garden, we got on the van, and my attitude was completely different. I felt relaxed, I felt nothing was bothering me. I just didn't care. I'm like, forget it, because it's not worth it. It's really not worth it. I was happy about that, 'cause I really don't want to go to jail just for hitting a kid. And I think he felt different too.

Now I'm waiting for everything to grow, so I can grab my vegetables and go home. Show my mom that I actually accomplished something in this program. You're calm with a garden. That's a feeling I like, being calm, relaxed. That's one way that life should be, you know. You don't push it past the point. You can't speed it up, you can't slow it down. You've got to let it grow by itself.

where we

come from

*M*y grandmother had nineteen girls and one boy. She had more than that, but she lost four or five I think she say. I was one of the grandkids. After the other girls got grown up and left, my grandmother brought me to Georgia to stay with her, 'cause I was living in New York with my mother. That's where I was born. My mother and another lady worked at a steel mill. This lady, Miss Alice, would keep me during the night, and my mother would keep her children during the day. This is the way I was raised up. 'Til my grandmother said, "No, no! I want my child down here with me. You're not going to raise her with white folks." Seriously, this is what happened! And so finally, my mother sent me down there to stay with my grandmother. I just fell in love with it, 'cause I could run in the fields and feel the earth and work on the farms and grow gardens—I had some of everything!

My grandmother was a caretaker in a big house, and we had a big vegetable garden. She always say, "We was made out of dirt—it all came from the earth." I said it couldn't, and she said, "Oh yes it did!" So that's when I started following her around. I worked right by her most of the time when she was gardenin'. And that's how I learned how to plant things.

I went to school down there and worked on the farm. From about nine to twelve we went to school, and then from there we worked in the fields the rest of the day, harvesting the vegetables. I tell you, one carrot, we'd make one meal out of it! We worked sharecrop on different farms. Not only for cotton and corn and peanuts, but we grew potatoes, collards, mustards, turnips, and rutabagas.

The earth, my grandmother taught us, is a healing medication. They would take the red clay and use it for medication if you got hurt. The white clay was something you'd eat if you got something inside. It cleans your blood out. Vitamins, minerals is in there. And iron and zinc is in clay too. You take a pick and chip your piece off and eat! Red clay the same way. My grandmother used to put it in the oven and  bake it. She'd put cinnamon and nutmeg and vanilla flavor on it, and we think we eatin' candy, sittin' on the porch—and it's earth!

If I can't get my hands in dirt, then I'll get sick. And it's true! 'Cause I'm out there digging in the dirt all the time. If I couldn't feel the earth in my fingers or my feet, then I might as well die, 'cause that's the way I've always been.

My life is mostly based on farming and African tradition. My great-grandmother came from Nigeria and my grandmother was born here. Back in those days when they came to this country, they came over on the slavery ship. My great-grandmother was named Feh-mi Jo-li-a-may. Jo-li-a-may is something like a god, one of their idols who they worship in Africa. They was not allowed to use their own name or speak their own language. So their name was changed from Jo-li-a-may to Thomas. And if they ever got caught speaking their own language they would be beaten.

We were never allowed to use our real name until the lifetime change—then you could say

who you were and where you came from. My great-grandmother was supposed to have been a hundred years old. And the work that I'm doing out there in the garden now, she did.

I studies while I'm working in the garden. A lot of time I pray and I studies. People say you can't do that, but I do. I'm a certified Sunday school teacher. I teach who's in the Bible and where they came from. Did you know that there was a lot of black peoples in the Bible? The greatest architect in the Bible was a black person. Nimrod, he was black. And Nineveh, in the Bible, he built all those cities. I studies this and I teaches this, and I tell them where they came from. Your main problem is, know who you are, where you came from, and how you got to be what you are today.

*W*ell, I really didn't want to work in a garden, period. When the lady first called and asked me to organize the garden, I told her no. I told her no three times. I said I promised my daddy I wasn't workin' on no farm when I left the South, and I'm not goin' out there. I always tell this story, that the day I walked out in the garden, I looked up in the sky, and it was like my daddy was lookin' at me. I said, "Dad, do you believe this?" And he said, "Yes, my daughter." He said, "You know, never be ashamed or afraid of what you done for a livin'." And that was just a release for me. I don't have to be ashamed of where I'm from. I don't have to be ashamed of what I've done for a livin'. I should take pride. He said if you don't know where you come from, you don't know where you're goin'. So I feel proud about where I'm comin' from.

To tell you the truth, when I first started out in the garden, a lot of my friends didn't want their neighbors to see them working in the garden, because a lot of them came from down South on farms. It was like a bad experience for them to be from the country. I used to let people know that bein' a farmer was nothin' dumb. You had to have some education on how to plan, how much fertilizer to use, how to plant seed, the whole bit. You couldn't just throw some seeds in the ground. And that was one of the main things that we had to do to let folks know that it was not a disgrace and not a shame to be workin' on a farm. The greatest gift that could have been given to us is to know how to garden. That's the greatest gift that anybody could give you, 'cause you can live. It's a gift, it's a trade. I let them know how wonderful it is to see your own creation when you put a seed in the ground, and see it grow!

"If you don't know where you come from,
you don't know where you're goin'.
So I feel proud about where I'm comin' from."

'**ve** been in love with a garden ever since I first seen my grandmother, Kattie Hannah's garden. I mean, she grew the biggest turnips. She would pull them fresh out of the earth. That earth was so rich and black. It was in Mississippi. She could pull them big ol' turnips out. Honey, I hated the way those things tasted. But honey, I loved to see them grow!

Her and my grandfather, Russell Hannah, had everything. They just had acres and acres. They grew sweet potatoes, watermelon, corn, squash. They had peach trees, everything! And that's what really put this in my heart, to want to be a gardener, because I seen what they were doing. It was just a miracle. You grow up with that and say, "My grandparents had everything, why can't I?" And that's why I try. I try hard. In Cleveland we got peach trees, we got sweet potatoes, they're growing in the yard. We got okra, beans, squash. We grew watermelons, just the little ol' tiny ones. The truth! I try to get the best I can out of this land we do have.

My mother, she taught us how to take that hoe and dig in the ground. One summer we were down South in Mississippi. And the mule would not gee and would not haw. He was a stubborn mule. He would not move. So Mama put that harness on me and my brother, and we pulled. My right hand to God—me and my brother, Bobo, we pulled that plow! They grew some great big ol' cabbage out of that soil, honest to God. When you got to eat, you will work. Honey, I mean, we became the mule that day. We broke that soil up, and we planted. We did! And we ate. It ain't been easy, but still God brought us out. He brought us out.

*E*ven though I didn't do it, I was still a part of it. I grew up around this. I guess you could call that a learning process. Who was that, Shakespeare, who said that we all are part and parcel of everything we see and hear and meet. It's a part of us whether it's good or bad. So I think that the garden is just a part of what I seen.

One of the things that I remember most is going into the garden and getting a tomato. It's ripe and you just take and wash it off and you eat it. My mother and my aunt would go out in the garden and get corn and peas and beans. We had a woodstove kitchen and it was hot! I'd watch them do things. They could go out in the garden, get all of these things and put a dinner together in nothing flat. Today I wonder about it when people have electric stoves, microwaves, gas stoves, and they got timers on them—all they got to do is turn the knob, and still they're tired. Yet, these people did it that way, and it was hot and they got it done. Those are the most beautiful things I remember—how they could do this.

In those days, Mississippi, Alabama, Georgia, Tennessee, even Louisiana, in fact, most of your southern states were predominantly agrarian. This is how they lived. And that's why those states were so poor. When you come into this neck of the woods, where you have your steel and your iron, there's more money here. But in farming there's very little money.

When I got older and started going to school and reading about other places, I thought if I left Columbus, Mississippi, if I could get to Memphis, that would be heaven! Oh yes, I thought about that. People go and they come back and talk about it. And then next was St. Louis. Boy,

I'll tell ya' that's a big-time town! And then Chicago. New York. Detroit. All of the big cities. And people would come back, and they had worked in the mills and had made quite a bit more money, even though they didn't understand that they were given a low job. I'm talkin' about blacks now. They were given the dirt jobs, but it was more money than what they were getting paid back South. Well, if

you don't know any better, it doesn't bother you. But when you know something, then it begins to . . . See, knowledge is a wonderful thing, but it can also bring on pain. It can bring on pain, because the more you know, the more bothersome it becomes in the mind—your mind worries.

Around 1960, I was headed for California. But I came here and got a job at Republic Steel. All the black people were put in the coke plant, the open hearth. That's where the smoke and the gases are. Most of the guys who died, died of silicosis of the lungs, from breathin' all of that stuff. I got a job in the coke plant 'cause me and my girlfriend got married. So now I had to do something. My wanderlust was gone, over with. So I stayed here in Cleveland. I got friends here, children, everything. I always think about Mississippi, though. I got a sister and aunts and cousins. I go there once in a while. It's hard to forget where you came from.

I noticed when I was workin' a lot of the people from Europe always talked about the old country. The old country, you can't get rid of that, it's part and parcel of you. Maybe fate didn't go too well for you, but you remember some of the happy times, some of the wonderful people

"It's all about
findin' your place in
the world."

you knew. You don't forget your roots. I used to hear them talk about the old country. They always called people DPs—a displaced person is a person without a country—but I quit doin' that. And then I hear people talk about Georgia and Mississippi and Tennessee, and we all get together and start talkin' about it. This is what it's all about. It's all about findin' your place in the world. And even though you thought you found a place, you find another place. There's still a place inside of you you can't get out of—you can't get it out.

If I were to leave here and go to California now, I'd always think about Cleveland. It's a part of you. It isn't a thing you can rub out like a pencil eraser. You know you can't just say phwoooosh, and it's gone. You can't do that. And yet you have your hard times, your good times, your bad times, and your sad times. This is really the only story I got.

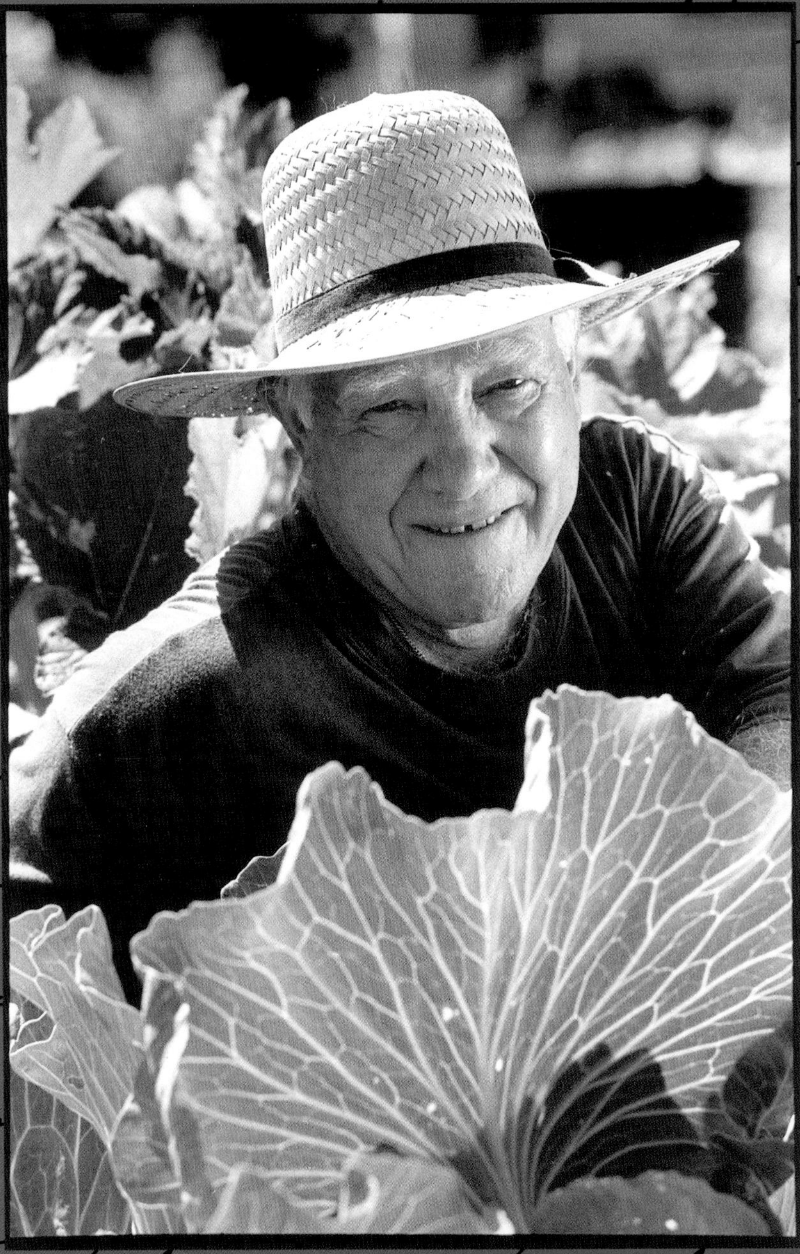

the prayer

garden

You have to nurture vegetables just like you do a child. I go so far as to even talk to them. I say, "Okay now, what are we going to do today? You've been good today!" One lady was looking at me and she said, "Are you all right?" I say, "Yes, I talk to flowers too." I have beautiful flowers. I say, "Are you going to be beautiful today? What are you going to do? Oh, do you guys want a drink? I'll give you a drink today." You think I'm nuts? This is what happens, you know, in growing.

I pray and I talk to them. I do. And I sing. I sings while I'm working in the garden. I've been singing all my life. I been singing with my church and my grandmother and family. We would sing as though we had our own choir. We would sing gospel songs—there was no jazz. When I came back to New York to live with my mother, that's when somebody enticed me to sing jazz, since they say I had a beautiful voice. So I started singing in New York. Then I left New York and came to Cleveland. There used to be a Club Oasis and I used to sing and do gigs in there. But God changed me and told me that I was a child of his and I had to let somebody else enjoy the talent that I had. So that's what I been doing since then, singing in the church.

Well, let me tell you what happened to me one day. I was out there singing in the garden. Just workin' and plantin' and transplantin' and singin'. I was having a good time by myself! I turn around, and people was there. Oh my God! I was so embarrassed. They said, "Don't stop." I had to quit and start laughing. "How long y'all been standing there?" I asked. "Long as you been workin', goin' up the way."

"I pray and I talk to them.
I do. And I sing. I sings
while I'm working in the garden."

*A*ll of us grandchildren and my aunties each had a little plot in my Grandfather Potts's garden, not quite an acre. That's what we had to do. Grandfather Potts was a carpenter. His name was Gibson Emerson Potts, but everyone called him Gip. He moved houses, jacked up houses on logs and moved them. Gardening and fishing was his joy, relaxation. His living was moving houses. He was a reverend too. He'd get out and walk around in the garden, think about his sermon. "Don't call me a farmer, I don't farm," he'd say. He gardened. He used to say that's the way he and me is getting in touch with God.

As a kid, I wouldn't go barefoot until I was in the garden. I've always been down to earth. I still am. That's where all the nourishment comes, through the earth, through my feet.

Anything you have that's alive needs attention—without attention it won't grow. You ever seen rain fall on a leaf? Before it goes anywhere it stops. It's giving it some attention. When you water plants, move your hands around so that it do just like the rain.

Every morning I get up and open the door, get the air in the back door and front. Let nature in. I wake up with joy. You can't give it to me. You got to earn it from God. He gives it to you, but you got to accept it.

"Every morning I get up and open the
door, get the air in the back door and front.
Let nature in. I wake up with joy."

*S*o this is the way it is with gardening. Gardening has been like a way out for me. You get out there, and you're just out there with the bugs and the birds and the bees. And then they don't bother you too much. You know, bugs they sort of crawl on ya' a little bit, but I can accept that. You get out there, a little bit of solitude. I think a fella should have a little bit of solitude, a little time where he can get out by himself.

t's so important to be present to people. For me sometimes it's just to be out in the garden. The garden is much more deep than just planting things. But even then, at the end of the growing season, we put out our little stand with all the tomatoes on it for people to help themselves. Our joy is that ultimately we'll be giving it away to somebody. It's all God's, and all God asks us to do is take care of it for a while. But keep giving it away, don't hold on to it.

As we know in the garden, if you don't harvest it, it's sad. It's sad to put all this time and effort and work into a garden and then let it sit and rot. That's heartbreaking. Let's harvest it! It's meant to be harvested. It's almost another sign of our society, where if people keep too much they get greedy. But when they give away of themselves they find life. If you're holding on to anything and fearful that someone's going to take it from you, you'll never discover the real joy in life.

It's always interesting to me in the spring. There's excitement. Everyone wants to get in the garden, and all the people come today and want to get everything in the ground. And I do too. But then come around July, all of a sudden that interest wanes and the weeds take over. And the hardest part is the commitment, and now they have to stay with it.

That's what's good about gardening. It teaches you discipline. You can't plant a garden without discipline. It also brings a certain order where there's chaos. You can't be a gardener without hope. And you know if you hope, the seeds will come, and they will bring life. You know all

"At the end of the growing season, we put

voices

out our little stand with all the tomatoes on it

for people to help themselves."

81

"You can't be a gardener without hope. . . . Just do what you can as best you can, and let it go."

that God ever asks of us in life is not to be successful, but to be faith-
ful. So that's all that matters. Just do what you can as best you can,
and let it go. If it works, it works, and if it doesn't, it doesn't.

e and my mother, we would go in the prayer garden and tell each other our deepest secrets. Just me and my mother. I'm a deaconess, and I've been consecrated for eight years at St. Paul A.M.E. Zion. People tell me their most deepest secrets in their lives, and I never tell anyone. I never reveal them. Never. We go in the prayer garden, and we sit on that little bench back there. We sit on the bench and we talk. Our most deepest secrets we tell each other, and our most deepest dreams, and hope that God will bring them to pass. Most of them come true, but we keep them sacred and secret.

A lot of things will come to me through the Holy Spirit. God will put it in my mind. And a lot of time I dream. When I dream I can see these beautiful gardens. I just go out there in the garden and God will guide me. I was reading about George Washington Carver, how close he had got to God. He said when you're in your garden, that's one of the times when you're closest to God. He'll just take you over and you can . . . it's just amazing what things you can do, because, see, God's working through you. You're not doing it. We're doing it here in this physical world, but God's the one that's doing it. If I was to just go out there and just start doing stuff, I could never have done anything like that. Honestly, it'd have to be God. It'd have to be.

came to the City Mission in 1996, homeless, after a divorce. I really didn't know too much about what the City Mission programming was. I thought it was basically a shelter for homeless individuals with a background in alcoholism or drug dependency, which wasn't the case with me. And lo and behold I got here and found out that the program is basically to introduce individuals to a Christian way of living.

And then I found that they had a garden program here. It's not really a gardening program to, per se, feed the people here at the City Mission or the homeless. But it's a program that we use to get in touch with spirituality, because gardening is very close to godliness. You know, when you plant a seed, and then you watch that seed grow into a vegetable, that's God's creation. This is the same thing that the City Mission does with these lives. We plant seeds as a way to Christianity. And then we see what the outcome is, and that's God's blessing. So that's basically what we do with the garden.

We have different people that come through with an assortment of different problems. So the garden provides a surrounding for one's peace and tranquillity. We'll have Bible studies in the garden and various meetings in the garden. And then certain individuals will go to the garden just to do their homework or their Bible study. So, it's a nice thing to have, 'cause it's a thing of beauty—and what's more precious and what's more beautiful than to be sitting in a garden? You know it puts you in a tranquil situation as far as your mindset. It gets you in touch with your spirituality.

voices

"Gardening is very close to godliness. You know, when you plant a seed, and then you watch that seed grow into a vegetable, that's God's creation."

You have a lot of time to reflect over your life when you're sitting in that garden. I used to go out in the garden very early, like six o'clock in the morning, and water before the sun would come up. Sometimes you could go through the trials and tribulations of the day and you could take yourself in your garden and get lost. You're weeding, but your mind may be a million miles away. That garden puts you in contact with something positive. When you come out of there, you've forgotten about all those problems or disagreements with people. I'll say people, 'cause people cause problems, you know. It's a good way of getting some peace and tranquillity. That's why I became interested in it. Course, I hadn't any, what you would say, experience as far as gardening.

Now I'm staff maintenance. I oversee whatever they do in the garden. You know it's not easy for the guys. When people come, we don't know exactly what has happened in their life. And just to see the changes and letting the garden be a tool to help them along—you know, it's really beautiful. You can feel it. It's just like a plant growing. When you put the seed in the ground, you don't actually see it, 'cause you have to go to sleep. Then when you wake up, you say, wow, look it! Before you know it you got a plant standing this tall, but you never see it grow.

Sometimes one of our counselors will take a group and they'll go out in the garden. I think that garden somehow or other has a tendency to make people open up. Whereas if you were in a classroom, there are certain things that are just not conducive to you opening, to saying what's really on your mind, or as they say, "what's really happening." But sittin' out there in that garden, what's really happenin' is happenin'. It's just divine intervention from God is how I can explain it. It's a difference in the surroundings and the setting. The garden has the ability to make people comfortable. When you go out there you start thinking beautiful thoughts. Evilness will leave you because you're in a beautiful environment. That's the way I look at it. These guys go out there and the garden changes their mind. They have all these problems, yet still they're surrounded by beauty. That sort of

changes them. And it's in the middle of "the bricks"! I never would have thought that I would have been involved in a garden situation. But being involved in this program, I thank God for that, because God put that in the plan.

I was employed by the city of Cleveland in the water department as an engineer. I made quite a bit of money, and I wasn't happy. Growing up we're taught that in order to be successful and happy in life, you get married, you have two kids and a family, a house, a new car, and you're supposed to be happy. It really didn't work out that way. You know I couldn't make enough. I took every opportunity to work overtime. The more you get, the more you want. And that which you did achieve is no longer meaningful. It means nothing. We aspire to drive different high-class cars. But what is a car? After I drove a Lincoln Continental, the novelty wore off, so it was nothing.

We don't make much money around here, but the rewards are beneficial. You can't equate that to money. So now I got a Ford Escort, and it does the same thing that my Lincoln did,

because my priorities are different. And that's what's important to me. In the garden, every year, you go through the same process over and over again, and you see the miraculousness of the growth. It's an ongoing experience. The novelty doesn't wear off. And that's the difference, because it's God's creation. Man makes cars, but God makes that seed turn into a fruit. And it's nourishment—nourishment not only for the body, but for the soul, for the mind.

afterword

*G*ardeners love to tell stories. We knew that much, because one of us—Lynn, who works with the urban gardening program in Cleveland—couldn't help but recount the stories she'd hear of Brenda Taylor's prayer garden, Dan Kane's amazing flat Dutch cabbage, or Steve Cernan's technique for mulching his tomato beds. We began to wonder if we could somehow record these stories for others to hear. Our combined skills as writer and gardener would complement each other in this effort, but could we manage to gather and arrange their stories without distorting their voices? It would be necessary to have the gardeners' trust in order for them to talk openly with us.

We tried first by asking gardener Gustina Nicholas if we could "interview" her. One warm, sunny February day we found ourselves at her kitchen table, drinking coffee and tasting the delicious muffins she'd baked for the occasion. We talked, listening to her stories about her neighborhood, her memories as a child gardening with her grandfather, her philosophies. We scribbled as fast as we could. The subject was gardening, but we followed the lively digressions of good conversation, talking with Gustina for an hour and a half. As we stood on her porch to say goodbye, she gave us a big, tight hug, and said, "I come from a family that gives hugs." This gesture set a tone that would become familiar to us.

We were excited about her stories, but realized we had lost some of Gustina in our hasty scribbling and penciled notations. So we went from our notepads to a tape recorder and began to talk with more gardeners. We had a growing sense that these stories were vital and important for others to hear. Time and again we felt lucky to be brought into the lives and experiences of these remarkable people. We always found Gustina's generosity echoed in different ways.

The only thing missing was images of the gardeners to accompany their stories. So we approached Cleveland photographer Don Snyder, who had volunteered in the past to take photographs for the urban gardening program. A community gardener himself, Don immediately shared our enthusiasm for the project. He began to meet the gardeners and found ways to capture their energy and passion for gardening in photographic portraits.

Meanwhile, we continued talking with more gardeners. In transcribing their interviews we took what originated as a dialogue and sifted out our own comments and questions that often prompted their stories. We didn't change their words or phrases, but edited and rearranged passages in an effort to recapture the effect of the oral story and convey its power on the page. Then we brought the edited stories back to the gardeners for changes and final approval.

Throughout this project we found inspiration from a booklet compiled by Cathrine Sneed about The Garden Project. This booklet contains the photos and thoughts of former prisoners she gardens with on an eight-acre organic farm in San Francisco. In addition, H. Patricia Hynes's book, *A Patch of Eden: America's Inner-City Gardeners,* encouraged us with new insights. Hynes documents the urban gardening movement in several cities throughout the country, often quoting the comments of the gar-

deners. She concludes her book with an impassioned call for us to "listen to the gardeners whose stories may hold more strategic and political power than the rigor of quantitative data."

Beyond the guidance from the books by Sneed and Hynes, the professional artistry of Don Snyder's photos, and our own efforts, this book would not have been possible without the generosity of the Cleveland gardeners. Not only did they openly share their experiences, but seldom could we leave an interview without first accepting a gift from the garden—a bag of tomatoes and string beans, or Egyptian onions to plant, then harvest all winter long. In their concern for their communities and with their open spirits, these gardeners speak for urban gardeners across the country. Their stories provide us with the most enduring bounty.

David Hassler & Lynn Gregor

95

afterword

profiles: the gardeners

Annie Browning loves to garden. She says if she couldn't feel the soil in her hands every day, she'd die. She was born in New York but as a child spent several years on a farm with her grandmother and great-grandmother in Georgia. This experience has instilled in her a lifelong passion for gardening. She is greatly involved with her church, where she's a Sunday school teacher and leads the Lydia Missionary Circle, which feeds and clothes the homeless. She is also a visitation minister and leads Bible studies at her home. Annie has a great talent for singing. She used to sing jazz, but now sings spiritual songs in the Mount Sinai Baptist Church Choir.

Steve Cernan was born in Bellaire, Ohio, and moved to the Tremont neighborhood in Cleveland when he was ten years old. His family grew a vegetable garden from two-cent seed packets that were available during the Depression. Their entire backyard was a vegetable garden. He studied horticulture at West Technical High School and graduated in 1935. In 1950 Steve started his own landscape business, which his sons now manage. For thirty-five years he worked in the National Guard, in charge of the Missile Defense in Cleveland. He and his wife, Betty B. Cernan, have been married for fifty-five years and spend nearly all of their time gardening in their vegetable and flower garden along Interstate 90.

Emmanuel Delgado is sixteen and was born in Cleveland, where he has lived all his life. His mother has been a great influence and has passed her knowledge of gardening on to him. He attends Max S. Hayes Vocational High School, where he is interested in learning the construction trade. Emmanuel also enjoys drawing, art, and reading comics. He participated in the Cuyahoga County Juvenile Court's Day Treatment Program. Besides receiving counseling and taking classes, the kids in this program have the option of gardening one hour a week.

Tommy Dorsey gardened occasionally when he was young. In 1996 he entered the City Mission, whose program reintroduced him to gardening. A place of Christian ministry, the City Mission welcomes men who need help and have no other place to go. Recently promoted to the position of assistant facilities manager at the City Mission, Tommy feels that the people there are like his family. He says it's a special place and that God brought everyone there together for a reason.

Julie Jackson began her work at the Children's Aid Society as a cottage parent. She is now the garden coordinator and works with foster children, many of whom have been abused. She also teaches nature study in the classroom. Besides her work at Children's Aid Society, Julie has two children and assists their teachers at school in gardening and nature/science activities. Julie is a member of the Olmsted Falls Garden Club.

Linda Jakob became interested in gardening as a child when she planted a sunflower seed in her parents' garden. She had to leave home for six weeks and, when she returned, she was amazed to find a huge, six-foot-tall plant. The transformation of a tiny seed into a huge plant has amazed her ever since. Linda has been a teacher at Joseph F. Landis School in Cleveland for ten years. She began planting seeds with students in her classroom, and this work eventually developed into an outdoor vegetable garden.

Dan Kane has lived his entire life in Slavic Village in Cleveland and is a retired Cleveland policeman. Rooted in his community, Dan has been a member of the St. Stan's Dad's Club since 1960 and started the Little League at

Morgana Park in 1960. Dan is the leader of the first city Summer Sprout garden, which began twenty-five years ago as a result of his idea to garden with youth in a crime prevention program.

Eugene Mattox has his own community garden and generously assists many other gardeners in his neighborhood. Although he had no direct experience as a child with gardening, he grew up in Mississippi surrounded by farms. He has eight children and fifteen grandchildren and spends his free time either gardening or taking part in church-related activities. He is a deacon at Second Tabernacle Baptist Church and teaches at other churches and at private homes.

Gustina Nicholas was born in Baton Rouge, Louisiana, and has lived in Cleveland for thirty years. She serves her community in numerous ways as a member of the Forest Hill Community Block Club and on the board of Neighborhood Housing. She volunteers in a variety of programs at her church and has been gardening with people of all ages in the Summer Sprout program for seventeen years. She says she's "grandmother for all the kids around."

Father Jim O'Donnell and **Maggie Walsh-Conrad** are cofounders of the Little Brothers and Sisters of the Eucharist, a contemplative community that lives a life of prayer. Father Jim, a Roman Catholic priest, and Maggie, a consecrated laywoman, have lived on East 35th Street for twenty years. They minister to youth in the neighborhood and in the Juvenile Detention Center, and to women at the Northeast Pre-Release Center. It is a common sight to see the neighborhood children working in the garden or playing in the large yard next to Father Jim and Maggie's house.

Brenda Taylor-Rosario was born in Mississippi and came to Cleveland in 1954 at the age of two. In 1989 she was consecrated as a deaconess at St. Paul African Methodist Episcopal (A.M.E.) Zion Church. Brenda believes she is set aside to do God's work. She has been a precinct committee member for fourteen years and has spent a few years as a volunteer at the Rockefeller Greenhouse. She has gardened her entire life and is a longtime Summer Sprout garden leader.

Dorothy Zeigler has been the leader of the Shaffer-Miles Community Garden for sixteen years. The garden has eighty members. She began gardening as a child in Mississippi. She is a widow and has six children and nine grandchildren. At Shaffer United Methodist Church, across the street from the garden, she is the chairperson of the Administrative Council and a lay leader who assists the pastor. Her other interests include line dancing and taking classes at Toastmasters, a public speaking group. Her charisma in public speaking can be seen when she speaks passionately about the community garden she leads.

Other gardeners pictured but not named in text: Letha Kvet with Dan Kane in the garden (p. 13); Thomas Weathers and Dan Pendleton in the corn (p. 20); Willie Pruitt (far right) and William Nizer (Dorothy Zeigler's grandson in stroller, p. 23); Justin Olszen, Anthony Hardin, and Ramanita Edwards with Linda Jakob (p. 48); José S., Betty T., and Lekeyshia D. with Julie Jackson (p. 52); Clifton Ware (seated, p. 70).

additional
information

Urban gardening began in this country in earnest around the end of the nineteenth century, when Detroit implemented a community gardening program as a way to supplement the food supply of the unemployed. Several major cities implemented school gardening programs in the early twentieth century. During the Great Depression of the 1930s and World War II in the 1940s the government sponsored gardens as a way for people to produce inexpensive, high-quality food. As the twentieth century progressed, the popularity of urban gardens waxed and waned.

The 1970s brought a resurgence of urban gardening which continues to grow stronger today. As always, there is still a need for urban dwellers to have fresh produce, green space, and a connection to the land.

And increasingly today, gardening is recognized as a healing activity. In the 1970s the federal government allocated block grant funds to twenty-three major cities in the United States to support community vegetable gardening. There are a variety of organizations that support and assist community gardeners by providing resources and education. In cities across the United States, notable community gardening organizations such as Cabrini Greens in Chicago, the Greening of Harlem Coalition, Roses in Roxbury in the Boston area, and Busy Bee Gardens in North Philadelphia empower people to care for a piece of urban land—pick up trash, excavate rubble from beneath the soil surface, plant seeds, harvest produce, and ultimately take responsibility for their neighborhoods.

The American Community Gardening Association (ACGA) was established in 1979 to promote the growth of community gardening and greening in urban, suburban, and rural America. A national organization, it helps community gardening programs get started by providing information about established programs and available resources. According to the ACGA, 350 community gardening programs exist nationwide.

In the Cleveland urban gardening program, many forces are at work. The city of Cleveland's Division of Neighborhood Services Summer Sprout program began in 1976 through federal block grant funds. Currently, the Cleveland urban gardening program is a cooperative effort of the Summer Sprout program and Ohio State University Extension's urban gardening program in Cuyahoga County. The program's mission is to develop and improve vegetable gardening, thereby improving the nutrition of low-income families and individuals. In 1997, the program sponsored 180 gardens, with over 2,300 gardeners participating on about forty-two acres of land in Cleveland. The Summer Sprout program provides seeds, plants, humus, fertilizer, rototilling, signs, and use of a fire hydrant for watering. O.S.U. Extension provides guidance, support, training, and education to the gardeners.

Each community vegetable garden typically has a leader who runs the day-to-day operations, and each garden group is autonomous, setting up its own rules and layout. The land used for gardening is owned either by the city or a private owner, or is leased from the board of education. Many gardens are connected to street clubs, or churches, and nearly every gardener shares his or her produce with neighbors or hunger centers. Gardens start in neighborhoods when people come together and want to start a garden.

The characteristics of the gardens are as varied as the people who live in our urban areas. They range in size from 4,000-square-foot vacant lots to two- to three-acre lots on school property. The number of people tending the individual gardens ranges from 5 to 120. There are gardens in neighborhoods, at schools, at nursing homes; there is a garden in the courtyard at the Juvenile Detention Center. Surrounded by brick and blacktop, the teacher guides the juveniles in planting their vegetable plants in spare tires. With resourcefulness and ingenuity, urban gardeners find no limits to where and how they can garden.

The following is a list of resources—books and organizations—to help you learn more about urban gardening or start your own community vegetable garden.

organizations

American Community Gardening Association (ACGA)
100 North 20th Street, 5th floor
Philadelphia PA 19103-1495
215-988-8785
e-mail: acga@ag.arizona.edu
http://ag.arizona.edu/~bradleyl/acga/acga.htm
The ACGA is the most comprehensive community gardening organization in the United States. This organization can help you locate a community gardening program in either rural or urban areas.

American Horticultural Therapy Association
362 A Christopher Ave.
Gaithersburg MD 20879-3660
1-800-634-1603

The Garden Project
Pier 28
San Francisco CA 94105
415-243-8558

National Gardening Association
180 Flynn Ave.
Burlington VT 05401
1-800-538-7476
http://www.wowpages.com/nga/home.html

community gardening programs

The following is a limited list of programs in a few major cities. Although most major cities have several programs, only one from each city is listed here.

Atlanta Urban Gardening
1757 Washington Rd.
East Point GA 30344
404-762-4077
e-mail: uge1121e@uga.cc.uga.edu

Boston Urban Gardeners
46 Chestnut Ave.
Jamaica Plain MA 02130
617-522-1259

Common Ground Garden Program
University of California
Division of Agricultural Sciences
L.A. County Cooperative Extension
2 Coral Circle
Monterey Park CA 91755
213-838-4540

Green Chicago
Chicago Botanic Garden
PO Box 400
Glencoe IL 60022-0400
847-835-8254

Green Guerillas
625 Broadway
New York NY 10012-2611
212-674-8124
e-mail: ggsnyc@interport.net

Growing Boulder
3619 W. 32 Ave. #9
Denver CO 80211-3155
303-413-7248
e-mail: veithv@ci.boulder.co.us

Cultivating Our Community
Ohio State University Extension, Cuyahoga County
2490 Lee Blvd., Suite 108
Cleveland Heights OH 44118-1255
216-397-6038
http://www.bright.net/~gardens/

Penn State Urban Gardening Program
4601 Market St., 2nd floor
Philadelphia PA 19139
215-560-4166

Portland Community Gardens
Portland Parks & Recreation
6437 SE Division St.
Portland OR 97206
503-823-1612
e-mail: pkleslie@ci.portland.or.us

additional information

Seattle P-Patch Program
  Department of Neighborhoods
  700 Third Ave., 4th floor
  Seattle WA 98104-1848
  206-684-0264
  e-mail: barbara.donnette@ci.seattle.wa.us

Toronto Food Policy Council
  277 Victoria St., Suite 203
  Toronto, Ontario, Canada M5B 1W1
  416-392-1107
  e-mail: FPC@web.apc.org

Urban Harvest
  PO Box 980460
  Houston TX 77098-0460
  713-880-5540
  e-mail: wkelseyl@aol.com
  http://www.jumpnet.com/~arjun/Urban Harvest/

books

Boston Urban Gardeners, Inc. *A Handbook of Community Gardening.* Edited by Susan Naimark. New York: Charles Scribner's Sons, 1982.

Hynes, H. Patricia. *A Patch of Eden: America's Inner-City Gardeners.* White River Junction, Vt.: Chelsea Green Publishing Co., 1996.

additional information